Praise for *Substance, Oblivion & Infinite Communion*

I come to the poetry of Jake Berry with open arms, holding out my hands in the spirit of trust as I listen to his experience of the infinite. Berry has always been our 20th and 21st Century visionary poet who joins with such luminaries as Julian of Norwich and Thomas Merton in approaching the ineffable. With integrity and a deftness that resists attention to the poet himself, Jake Berry narrates a purely natural beauty, observing "the man across / the street / tending / his tea roses." The poet brings us an encompassing sacrament with signature deftness in such graceful passages as "the inscrutable calligraphy / of a ballerina." Always attuned to the inherent holiness in experience, Jake Berry reconciles substance with oblivion in a brave declaration of communion as the most fundamental reality.

Sheila E. Murphy – author of *Escritoire*

"We were talking about/ the collapse of time/ like a dried corpse/ crumbling into its shell." In his latest collection, Jake Berry invites us into the Infinite. Not as transcendent argument, but as Being. As arrival that has always been there, if we only know how to look. The poems here follow a consistent impulse in Jake's work that insists on the faithful transcription of what comes in from degree zero. I am always brought into the company of Keats and Spicer when I read Berry's work, a heady, exhilarating attunement. Go on, tune in yourself. See what's waiting this side of "Oblivion/ and love's/ implacable light."

Tim VanDyke – author of *Memoir of My Assassin's Body*

This is a powerful and unforgettable poetry collection. It is bold, original, and deeply thought-provoking. By blending religious insight with scientific curiosity, mysticism with everyday life, the poet explores the mysteries of mind, nature, and time with striking imagination. Each poem offers lines that linger, challenging and expanding the reader's perspective. Moments of abstract imagery woven throughout deepen the experience, inviting reflection beyond words alone. What sets this work apart is its fearless vision and unique voice in capturing ideas that feel both vast and intimate. A rare and luminous collection, it speaks to the deepest questions of existence and leaves a lasting impression.

Mary Assel, author of *The Holy Quran Verbatim - An innovative Translation* and *A Sprinkle of Dust*

For some years Jake Berry has been steadily perfecting the workings of a language meant to encompass the vastness of answers beyond the temporal, while maintaining the affability of a trusted friend who is calmly moved to share the possibilities with you. With *Substance, Oblivion & Infinite Communion*, he arrives in the realm of perfect wonderment and easy transmission. Eternal underpinnings are recognized in the company of personal memory, and all is voiced with the same trust and loving intention. Throughout the book, both the irrelevance of Materialism and removal from tuggings of dogma are clear enough, with the radiance of patiently gleaned knowledge guiding the journey. In the end, we can take undeniable heart in the crystalline magic of the poet's language itself, which attains both a measured richness and sheer rarefication unsurpassed by any metaphysical poetry within my memory.

David Thomas Roberts

There is a deep and abiding sense of mystery at the heart of Jake Berry's poems in Substance, Oblivion & Infinite Communion, a sustained feeling of awe as "abyss / cries out to abyss / and the pulsing chambers / compose a liturgy // without words, / the river birds leaping / into the wind." What most moves me about Berry's work here is the way he finds in the "substance" of the material world— the world of nature, and the world of his Alabama home— the "infinite communion" that makes for a mystical poetry that is also homely and lovingly quotidian. Here, cicadas might be a "rare breed of angels," and we behold "stars in the mouths / of a flock of blackbirds." This book is a quiet miracle.

Norman Finkelstein

Notes on Substance, Oblivion and Infinite Communion

For those who are new to the works of Jake Berry, you are in for a rare treat. There are few among us who deserve the descriptor of genius. I have personally known only two and one has departed this world.

The works of Jake Berry are truly inspired and born of visions that are both visual and auditory. He is an artist and a musician as well as a poet. He is a philosopher as all true poets must be. He is a man of vision who seems always open to new worlds and inspirations. He is a man of the spirit. He feels deeply and sees beyond the surface of all things. He is a scholar whose knowledge of his art is bounded only by his knowledge of the world.

Substance, Oblivion & Infinite Communion was in the works for over three decades yet it predates Socrates. Its original source is an ancient philosopher named Anaximander who proposed that the infinite is the source of all things. I surmise that this infinitude would at minimum represent God. It may in fact be God. It is the all-force that Joseph Campbell proposed as the essence of universal mythology in that it is present in all religions.

Berry takes this concept and allows it to take any form it chooses within the confines of poetic expression. It is present in the shadows of trees, in the marrow of bone, in the doorways of thought, in the visions of dreams, in the reflections of light, in the mystery of being. He dives into the deep subconscious and beyond, far beyond, where words cannot reach. He dives into the absence, into the abyss, into the farthest reaches of oblivion. The mysterious becomes the mundane and the mundane reveals itself in mystery.

"…abyss cries out to abyss / and the pulsing chambers / compose a liturgy / without words."

Yet Berry finds words that allow us to take this journey with him. For it *is* a journey. It is an adventure of the heart, mind and spirit. It is an uncovering of the unknown. An exploration of the heart of darkness. And from this, visions appear.

"Burn these letters. / Burn them in / alabaster lamps / at winter floodtime."

We meet our hero standing by the river and she is as perplexed as we are. She is driven, as we are, to understand what cannot be understood. She is the observer as we are. She is the explorer.

"We were talking about / the collapse of time."

There is an ongoing dialogue between philosophers. They
are exploring the nature of time and space, of space in time,
of the impossibility of time existing without form. The
house is fractured. It comes into view and vanishes.

"And looking down for his hands / discovers that he too
has vanished."

There is love where none should be. Yet that is the nature
of love. Love and beauty. What right have they to exist?
And yet they do. They are inserted into our lives, our
ruminations, our understanding of all that is in the center of
being.

Christ rises from the ashes. "It is noon / and Easter hangs
/ waiting / to be taken."

"We were talking about the darkness of God."

The spiritual nature of this work hits like the hammer of
Thor. There is no escaping the essential religious core of
thought expressed here. We are forced to confront our
own religious leanings.

"The fear / of God / is the beginning / of Wisdom / and
death / is the beginning / of fear."

It is somehow a contest of God, Wisdom, Fear, Love and
Oblivion. I am reminded of the great mythological works
of William Blake – also a deeply spiritual individual. We
are dealing with issues of the grandest and most profound
nature. And yet ordinary matters of nature and humanity
acquire equal weight. We are after all sentient beings and

our senses are the conduits of all we perceive. Wisdom and profound moments approaching understanding almost stumble into our lives.

"We hear / a shaft of darkness / falling through / the daylight / of a dream / where death trembles."

Beauty asserts herself even in the dying of flowers, the ruined cities, the bodies of the dead, the abandoned homes. The sky, the sea, the earth, the sun are the substance of our lives. They live and they die as we live and perish. "Only beauty remains."

"No. The Source / precedes the silence / from which the wound / is born."

Ultimately we must deal with death. "We invented death / rather than live / with imponderable mystery." And yet death *is* the "imponderable mystery."

The poet's answer is that nothing really ever dies. It transforms in an infinite cycle. What is always has been and always will be. Everything we experience in thought, dream, feeling or the senses exists in perpetuality. Eternity. Always.

"We are at the beginning. We can relax now."

"The whole of it / floods back / so tenderly / that tears / would dilute / its gentle power."

"It is always before."

In the world of the poet, love conquers. In the universe of Jake Berry, love conquers but not without a prolonged struggle. Yet in the end, it is always before.

You are not likely to find a book that has so much to reveal about our existence. So much to say about who we are and why we are here. So much about time, space, purpose, spirit, life and understanding. He has once again achieved a rare triumph of human expression.

Substance, Oblivion & Infinite Communion is a book to be treasured, read and read again – perhaps years from now when we have gathered more knowledge and acquired greater wisdom.

Ray Miller

Substance, Oblivion
& Infinite Communion

Jake Berry

ISBN 979-8-9950386-0-3

Library of Congress Control Number: 2026909948

7 Points Press is a non-commercial enterprise dedicated to the promotion of poetry and all the arts principally in The Shoals Area of Alabama.

7pointspress.com

other books by Jake Berry

The Pandemonium Spirit
Idiot Menagerie
Hairbone Stew
Equations
Unnon Theories
Brambu Drezi – Book 1
Species of Abandoned Light
Phaseostrophes
Folk Tales
Brambu Drezi – Book 2
Sefer Viscera (with Jim Leftwich)
Scratching Face
Silence and The Hammer (with Wayne Sides)
Drafts of the Sorcery
Brambu Drezi – Books 1-3
Cyclones in High Northen Latitudes (with Jeffrey Side and Rich Curtis)
Outside Voices: Correspondence (with Jeffrey Side)
Genesis Suicide
Phaneagrams
Trilogy: Kenosis
The Oracle House

Introduction

This book originates more than 30 years ago when I initially encountered the pre-Socratic philosophers. Much more recently while attempting to organize my papers I ran across work from that period that referenced *apeiron*, a term used by Anaximander to describe the first principle from which all things rise and into which they return. Apeiron itself is eternal and infinite, literally meaning "without limit."

 It is unlikely that Anaximander was the first to propose the infinite as the source of all things. He lived in the 6th century BCE and there are earlier texts from Mesopotamia, Egypt, India and China that express a similar understanding. Following a few generations after Anaximander, Parmenides also proposed an eternal substance as the ground of being. Many philosophical and theological traditions were similarly persuaded including later Greek philosophy, Christianity, the various forms of Neoplatonism, Jewish mysticism and any number of other schools of thought all over the world.

Compelled by this ancient idea, I simply followed it wherever imagination and intuition led. The images arrived along with the poems from a similar impulse and belong to the same notebook. This work does not offer any sweeping theory about the nature of the infinite but arises instead from an experience of it. Nor do the poems describe a linear process moving from substance through oblivion to arrive at infinity. They are always simultaneously present and are themselves only words that inadequately express a reality that defies language. Yet when driven beyond their conventional limit words may disclose the potential that is the common heritage of all creatures – a shared communion in the infinity of existence.

Substance, Oblivion & Infinite Communion

Blue fire
 rises from a sundial.

Blue fire like a torch
 in late afternoon.

  The trees have become silhouettes,
 a language scribbled against the horizon.
    They speak to one another
   in old tree words,
      underground, in their roots,
     where the sun is going

 a point
  in the marrow.

If I close my eyes
a doorway moves
    out of the mist.

If I open my eyes
a massive impossible beast
    leans down
    to sniff for food.

    If I am dreaming
        should I walk
        through the doorway?

    If I am awake
    should I close
        my eyes?

What is this place?
        If I know it
 I know it by virtue of light.
     But if it is a place
        distinct from any other
  what is the nature of that light?

Each separate thing
       on the windowsill –
figurine, bottle, bell and painted stone –
  is an abyss in itself
 even if in this moment an abyss of light
    formed of this ever-reaching present
  into these particulars
     that seem to be perfectly at rest.

  The light will not leave them alone
but shifts as the clouds thin.

   The singular and multiple
    are the same presence,
     composing it even as they are composed
  by the scene itself
     which might be known
   only as they compose a mind.

We were talking about
the darkness of God.

"Snow through
dense fog…"

"We could not tell
land from sea from air."

"He fell on his face
on the deck of the ship
mumbling half forgotten
prayers into the damp
wood."

"This was before —
when order did not
exist."

"We are always before."

The persistent
absence
in the full-length mirror
at the end
of a long hallway
in grandmother's house

summons,
enchants,
empties the soul
of all those
who linger there.

The gold leaf
flaking from
a beaded frame

inscribes
every reflection
and those vacancies
in her light

demanding
oblivion

wash
you
clean.

"It's gone,"
    she whispered

  across
    hair thin
filament —

  a single photon,
  a piercing needle.

Within that point
   a swirling sea
 vast
 deep
 fathomless
   supernal.

And with a click
the kitchen appeared,
  butter,
  eggs,
  coffee,
  bacon,

the man across
 the street
tending
 his tea roses.

The void
  is a veil,

        appearing perfectly
      conformed
        and empty

     particle to particle
     house to house

with sisters weeping
in their blue robes
at Mother's door.

 She stood
motionless
on the other side
 gathered into herself

   but out of great pity
   opened the door.

      And Abraham paid
        by tithe and sacrifice
        an eternal priesthood

    as the siters
    crossed the threshold
    dancing

and in that dance

were perfectly annihilated

leaving only the song
  they heard

  as an echo,
     an excess

  measurable
    fluctuating

on the tongue
of every
   singsong being.

"alien to all things" *

in which
  no circumference
can be drawn,

  takes it measure
  breath by breath

  as he stands
   by the river
   waiting

  through a
   burnished red
afternoon.

                    *Maximus Confessor

Returning
    to before again

as everyone must
    if there is justice,
    if there is mercy,
    if there is wisdom
        and understanding
    and a crown of glory.

Before the gathered
    and anointed Word
set the foundations
    of the world
    and set them
        spinning
            in their core,

    the ladies
in their pastel dresses
and flower laden hats,
    the men
in seersucker jackets
with their hair greased back

    came to church
    of an Easter morning

with plates of vegetables
    canned last fall
and salted ham
from the winter hogs.

If their faces
    have grown obscure

beneath dust,
    decay and verdigris

        it is because
        no one sees
            a face

and doesn't live.

Four centuries
into the rape
of the Divine

the transparencies
were shimmering

speaking through
roots, chicken wire
and wireless code

the eschaton
of fever and
the fever of
brittle, intricate
noise

strewn like
tiny razor sharp
diamonds
across the forests.

But abyss
cries out to abyss
and the pulsing chambers
compose a liturgy

without words,
the river birds leaping
into the wind.

Burn these letters.
 Burn them in
alabaster lamps
  at winter floodtime.

They will glow
  black and dense
because their sources
  are the black traces
  that dance across
    the mind's conflagration.

We drown in nectar
  locked in amber,
    woven into
  the slumbering procession

    out of the fire
    coalescing into form
and form into
    muscle and bone

  gathering the ash
    of these letters
  into the chambers
    of a vast
  and infant heart.

Sunlight through
   stained glass.

The imposition
 of ashes
 from mussel shells.

40 days
dressed in white
chanting
the baptismal vows.

40 days
into the water.
   Those who enter
return uncreated.

Oblivion
 and love's
 implacable light.

She is standing
 beside the river
watching the current
   swirl and flow

with no memory
 of how she arrived.

She pulls the blanket
close around her.

The grass flickers
    in and out of form.

The far shore
    trembles, blurs and fades.

There was a tree
but the tree is gone.

She notices
she is hungry.

The sound of traffic
mangled with silence.

It reminds her
    of a voice.

It reminds her
    of a name,

whatever a name
    might be,

however sound
    might mean,

waves in the atmosphere.

Today is
 a black screen.

Today is
 a black screen
pocked with the
 flickering debris of love.

 A word is
 beating
the cloud brooding
 against the screen.

 He is driven
into the desert
 where wild beasts
and angels
 do their work

 and desire
shapes its
 jealous accusations.

The river of it
 will not leave her alone
standing motionless
 in the hushing noise.

Consider a feathered branch
  eloquently articulated
into a radiant drapery
  of fog and first light,
frost and bird song.

  The fingers of it know
    a paradox
    disclosed
    in the notes
    trilling back
      into nothingness.

The absurdity of it,
  veins grown out of the wood
like talons from stone,

  a shattering of mathematics
  in the sheer inscrutability
of what blood can do
    across the ages.

We were talking about
    the collapse of time

like a dried corpse
    crumbling into its shell.

"Time cannot withstand
the perpetual weight of the eternal."

'Time cannot bear the distance
because distance is purely formal."

"Can we say that form is incarnational
    and that incarnation is temporal?"

"Yes. It is a point of focus
    that depends on the observer."

"And who is the observer
    or does that remain hidden?"

"The observer is every point of form
    peering out of form toward the eternal."

"Every sensate form?"

"Every sensate experience."

"Every closed door eventually cracks."

"One house. Many rooms.
    But the house must be abandoned."

"And having abandoned the house,
                    time is forgotten."

"Not forgotten. Displaced. Fractured.
      It is even possible the fragments
      become superimposed."

"One feels like many?"

"Yes. Though none of them possess
   any fundamental existence, in their formality."

"One is many and many are none?"

"One is many and many are empty.
   There is no essential one since one is form."

"Yes, even before we begin counting
      form has competed its incarnation."

"The man looks up
   and the room has vanished."

"And looking down for his hands
      discovers that he too has vanished."

"It is always before."

Every hollow bone
   in the cemetery
seeds the fecundity
            of paradise

sweeter than honey
   in the comb,   sweeter than sunlight
they will rise   after a long night of rain
   one spring morning

while the birds
   are still sleeping   while the spirit
                                     nestles easy under the leaves

and only the soft
   rush of a woman
bearing rags   voices beneath
            and flowers   the swish of passing feet

   can fulfill
   the promise
whispered long ago
   by an old man dreaming

"The pity was earthly
    and the bliss was heavenly." *

and the water earth encloses
    is a fire in heaven

descending in showers
    where we played

  in the trellis,
    a disappearance game,

your face hidden
    in the leaves so well

I thought you were
    the spirit of the place

  humming in my skull
        a song in words

no one ever sang
    until I broke you free

and we tumbled downhill
            into the stream,

  a gentle nothingness
    to close the distance

  before the elements
emerged naked, baptized.

I am weeping
    for you still

even though you reside
    in every arch and neuron,

        a scruffy girl laughing
        with red clay hands.

                *Julian of Norwich

We are suddenly
   thrust outside the limits

   like a flock of birds
     on a cloudy day
   turning toward you
     seems to disappear.

It is a coat
   you cannot wear,
a name
   you cannot voice

as transient as moonlight
     caught in owl song

   the grounding night

   when every face
 is emptied
   of its grave.

They spoke for hours,

two women
  in antique ladder back chairs

    looking out
through dim, burnished light,
  caught in a room
    of soft objects

  in sounds
unheard

    since before
    the flood.

The bodies floating –

  then the absence
    of bodies.

  The hush
and the still water,

    the tones
in which they were speaking.

Sheol is empty.
    The pit is swept clean.

 Green saplings
rise from the floor.

    Luminous air
whispers through the leaves,

 "I am here."

It is noon.
    It is noon
  and the sun is eclipsed.

Where was time
  before it was caught
   in the increments
    that cling to the flesh
  of every living creature?

It is noon
  and Easter hangs
  waiting
    to be taken.

We were talking about
the darkness of God.

  We were hovering
over a battlefield

  a vast flowering garden.

  The harvest
is a sacrifice

  poured like a fountain
  across the ground

filtering down
  through the stone
and rubble
  and mountains of garbage
left by an errant species.

  The beauty of it
  is unforgiveable,
and more real
    than seeing.

"I am here,"
she said in her sleep
  and dropped the phone.

This is not the surface.

   "Surface
       beneath
           surface?"

   No.

The wild phlox
   coming into flower
are heaven's own.
Beneath them
    in the wet and loamy ground
  the surface
      embraces the roots.

   This is not the surface,
black marks on a white field.
  It is the trace of someone passing
  and fading in and out
    of a deeply immersive

  and fertile waking
    which is substance
  and the heart beneath.

Have you seen the hours
  planets and stars rolling
across the sea floor?

Have you seen them
  tumbling into fathomless
  chasms and disappearing?

No vast explosion.
No earthquake or storm.
No muffled cry
    in the distance.

  Have you seen
  a soft light shining
in the back room
  of a ramshackle house
    on the edge of a wood
  in the Georgian mountains?

  Have you looked
    inside and seen
    anything more
  than an empty house?

The fear
    of God
is the beginning
    of Wisdom
and death
    is the beginning
    of fear.

If perfect love
casts out fear
then perfect love
    robs death
    of its prey
and nothing remains
  beyond Oblivion

and Oblivion
is the beginning
    of God.

Smoke
  in an empty room

drifting

  around a rose
  suspended

  dissolving,
turning the smoke
  blood red.

 What could be
more impossible
than a windowless room
filled with red smoke

  where a rose
  used to be?

A day's skin
can give it away —

sunlight rippling
  through the feathers
and leaves

  disintegrating
whatever philosophy
  might entangle
among the insects
  passing through
  the dewy grass

who sing only
  what music ripens
in nerves
  and senses
    brought to flower.

What the cicadas reveal
  is more than
red eyes, black bodies
  and translucent rings.

  Their high pitched
  sonorous roar,
distant, immediate
  surrounding us

  might be that
  rare breed of angels
delivering a message
  as alien to them
  as they are to us.

Why do they feel strange
  in our eyes and ears?
Is the wisdom
  of a lifetime
  buried in the earth

  ominous, dreadful,
  disconcerting?
Are they asking
  a question we cannot answer?

  Let them roar,
and listen closely
  to the dark peace
  of things
  impossibly known.

Ceaselessly
  ceasing,

  I am,
  neither substance
  or void,
  the very imprint
    of Being –

    an image
with no place or time
  but immediately present
  everywhere and always
    in all things

  pouring out of nowhere
  the uprooting
    foolishness

  I am.

The horizon trembles,
    flickers
  and seduces
    with radiance
  I vanish
    to become.

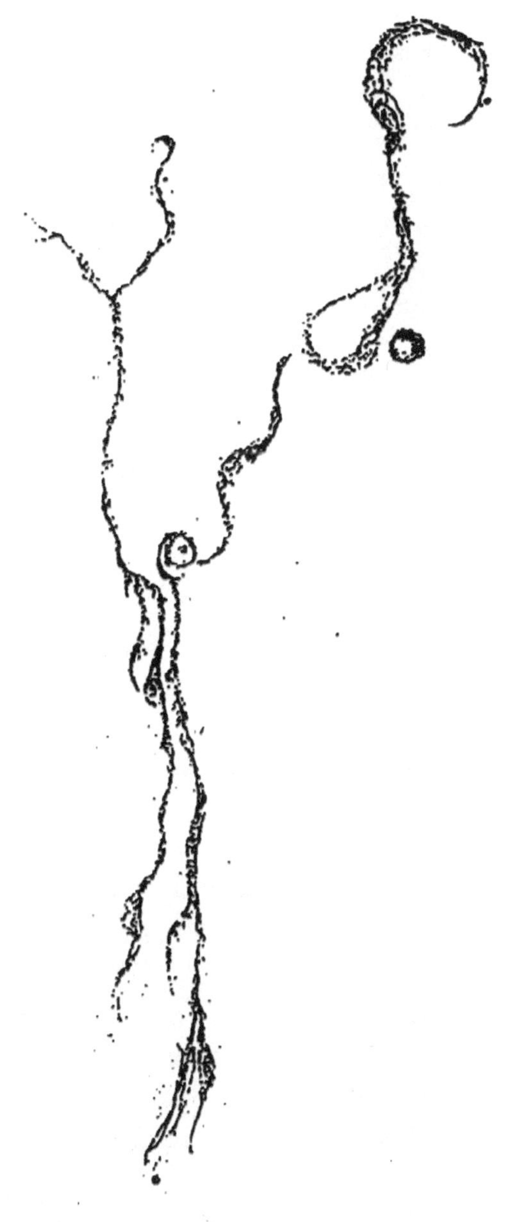

"These depths, they are Love." *

   All worlds are transparent,
    broken eggshells,
    beneath the gaze of the Lord.

  Her eye is altogether miraculous,
endlessly faceted,
   each facet spreading into
  a multitude of worlds.

The golden flower
   strikes at the air
  with every petal demanding
    substance and release
  whose surrender is beauty
  is pain is formlessness.

Out of the shell
   the image wakes, shakes her wet feathers
  and begs to be fed,
   Christ of the rocks
    crying aloud
     in stark prophetic creatures
  of bread and wine.

Come to the feast
   empty of all imagining
  and see the species gather
   to hear their first and only name.

   *Thomas Merton – New Seeds of Contemplation

The sky
all spring
  like
burnished silver

  reminded us
of a heaven
  we cannot remember.

Its crisp bells
  clanging
so deep
  in the blood

  we hear
  a shaft of darkness
falling through
  the daylight
of a dream

  where death
trembles.

"Time is the moving
 image of eternity."*

   whose imperfect features
 stream like quicksilver
    through your fingers
 binding the galaxies
 with such tenacious hunger
    for Being,

 groundless except for that
 motion toward the other,
    inexplicably drawn.

 The street vendor
    hawking his wares,
 the beetle constructing
    her home of dust and water,
 the fires in the veins
  of the earth,
 the bluebird and mockingbird
  at war on the wires
     emerge
     disappear
      and remain

  performing
    the light
 in which
    they are clothed.

                              *Plato – Timeas

Into the whiteness
darkness radiates

breaking the filament
of eternity wide open
and throwing the window open
at first light

but in the heart
darkness illuminates

she smells the wisteria
and honeysuckle

how effortlessly
the body swims
through the soul

and forgets her name,
the drift and weight
of her body
in the damp air

as if they were
attributes
of the same impulse

turning toward the light
to summon every being
completed in the arc
of perfection and return.

Then suddenly
after years of empty prayer
  thrust into the rushing
    heart of it.

 Water, like galloping horses
torn out of sky,
  a torrent through the nebula
  scattering the stars.

  Beneath her feet
    the grass is waking.
  The river is finding her current
and opening her mouth

    to devour the seabirds
  for their transgressions,
    to dismantle the hills
    for a song her people sang

 while they danced
  toward the temple
 in the golden light
  of the good Lord's moon.

Entering the temple

you hear the sound
of wind over water
sighing through the columns

the pulse
in the distance –
thundering –
fading –

echoes down the long
wine red halls,
echoes up through
the wires
shudders down to the bones
and mortar.

Absent
for a season, a season
and half a season

You return
with the taste
of smoldering coal
on your lips.

All flesh is grass
All grasping after the Spirit
  is vanity

  The room is empty,
  the walls, bare and pale.
  Someone is breathing
  through the odor of saffron

but there is no presence
    of form
   or time
     or disembodiment.

All of nature
 is a weird confabulation
   in a floating mirror,

a bet between
  the angel races
 on how swiftly
   love does her work

   with such coarse thread.

Only beauty remains
    in the dried, withering flower.

Only beauty remains
    in the ruined city,
        grass growing
    through cracks in the street,

in the abandoned chrysalis,
    the scarf caught in the wind,

    the fencepost with
        barbed wire hanging loose,

the line of carcasses
        waiting for the butcher,

the rough limestone
    submerged in the fountain,

the empty husk
    of a house at dawn.

Only beauty remains.

We have forgotten
   what water is.

 Bodies moving
     across the surface
   in the reflecting pool,
a slight breeze
   disturbing their forms.

This is the event horizon
     we name
     where angels bathe
   and the water remains
                    motionless.

 We have forgotten that
 we are fashioned of it
   in weird geometries

that make time ridiculous
   and space a plaything
 of fragmented, contingent beings.

  Where they splash and laugh
 the reflections morph
   and reflect nothing so real
 as the Maker's gaze.

  In those eyes
     we tremble and dive
  and drink and die
       and slip into what waits beyond.

They will smuggle you out
through abandoned warehouses
wrapped in muslin
with a candle on your chest.

They will pay the debt
to the incinerator,
a savior torn out of place,
a world on fire

falling weightless
and silent
into the space
your imagination conspires.

There are depths
  beneath the sky
  the sky knows nothing of.

  It beats in the pulse
of every creature
    who remembers the sea.

  He looks down into you,
the eagle you encountered on the road
  and sees and knows completely
what we can know nothing of.

  And taking it deeply in her pinions
      and skull
    shakes herself into its presence
  and carries it into flight.

  You feel the swift absence
  and stammering towards it,
    call it beauty

  and surrender
where the sky cannot go.

A long string of lights
   drawn across the plateau
   ignites the hemisphere

   stars in the mouths
of a flock of blackbirds.

To see beyond that thick net
   of feathers and that bleak, shrill cry,

   a single luminosity
   simpler still than One

   through which morning
   explodes into glory

   and the blind outshine
   every burning eye

   hungry to appear.

Three dimensions —
Your hand, gesturing forward,
    your face and green Pentecostal robes,
the red carpet behind you

  and a fourth,
the choir — music,
    ratio of sound in space
    through duration

and beyond them,
    the rail and the altar,

the feast,
    our origin
    and resolution

  initiation,
culmination,
  ek-stasis.

Thales was wrong.*

We sleep beneath
    great spreading chestnut trees
    while the squirrels scurry about
    and a slow rain falls.

  Water cannot make us
even though it lives in the seed.
    It is not soul,
  but soul refracted.

  The mind creates
  its own difficulties
    and curses the spirit
  that wakes it,

    slipping though,
  in streams beneath the ocean
    that imagination
  out of which it rises.

                    *Thales thought water was the primal element

When YHWH comes
haunting your prayers
like a wolf

head low
and hungry

grass withers
beneath his paws,

his warm breath
gathered for the kill
releases the seed
from its grave.

Marigolds, aster
and red clover
follow in his wake.

What is the substance
     of a pulse

in deep sea currents?

    Stella Maris
known by her children,
  their rough skin,
    like leather
      made by the sun and wind.

  Carry them back
    to their tribes
      in small boats
    made of tongues.

When she died
she did not leave her body

but went deep
inside herself

down a path
through the illuminated dark

following a massive
red bear

until she came upon
a trembling nest of eggs

the color of planets
caught in motion.

Licking the blade
    of a slaughter knife,

tasting the blood
    of another animal

    ignites a fire
    in the brain

    pouring out
across the landscape

    where it settles in stone
    and waits.

A garden made
of the scent of oranges
          and black olives

and sky
the color of blue porcelain

shimmering,
 burnished,

    one breath removed.

There is a wound
behind the tongue
    that fertilizes language.

    The tongue itself
is a mystery,
    a deviant oracle

(before the words
arrived fluttering
    with a song

    and talons
ripping the city
    from its hinges).

No. The Source
    precedes the silence
        from which the wound
is born

        dripping wet.

A boiling black cloud
    of beaks, talons and lightning –

 we invented death
rather than live

  with imponderable
mystery.

 The dust
tore our eyes apart,

  and blinded,
weeping black tears

until, beneath
    their shroud

 we glorified
absent tyranny.

And mystery,
  made absurd

  hovered brooding,
a mother whose distant call

  is her first
and constant song.

Light undulating
   from light

   multifoliate,
eternally dissolving –

   each leaf
a seraphic choir

revealing through
   impossible harmonies

   the fiery
disposition of joy.

They are speaking
    in the quiet rushes of the afternoon
by starlight.

    Her dress is made
of days and years and ages,
    soft white silk
    in descending folds

from worlds before
    and worlds to come.

You rise in phases
    and know
the darkness
    is alive.

From out of a cellar closet
a ray of shadow

   finds its form
and assumes the miracle

   breathing into his coffee
while finches arrive

      spread and fly
    into an unseen tree

waiting for the birth
   of a child
  wild enough

     to make it shine.

For everything that was lost
a disembodied trace remains.

  Across their tombs
mothers pace and weep

  and a river
  finds its source
beneath the broken concrete.

  The rubble speaks
rising in the heat
    inarticulate, brutally alive

stalking the penitential
    gods.

From the sloughs of paradise
  broken

into an infant universe
  flickering out
 of its shuttered gate

  a salamander
 is a kind of negation
    in fire

 craving only
 the body of a man.

Water is the circumference,

the fingerprints
    you leave on your ghost

like the inscrutable calligraphy
of a ballerina
        tracing the architecture of your days
    across the surface of a wave.

Should we continue to pursue
such rough, deliberate questions?

    like feathers
growing from a mossy stone?

    Spacetime trembles
and surrenders

     some geometry
absolutely otherwise.

After the portal.
After the arched doorway
   hung in a frame on the wall
comes the beginning.

   For those who wait
beside the doorway
      the beginning cannot exist.

It is an unknown possibility
      suggested by
an ornament on a wall

   in no particular place.

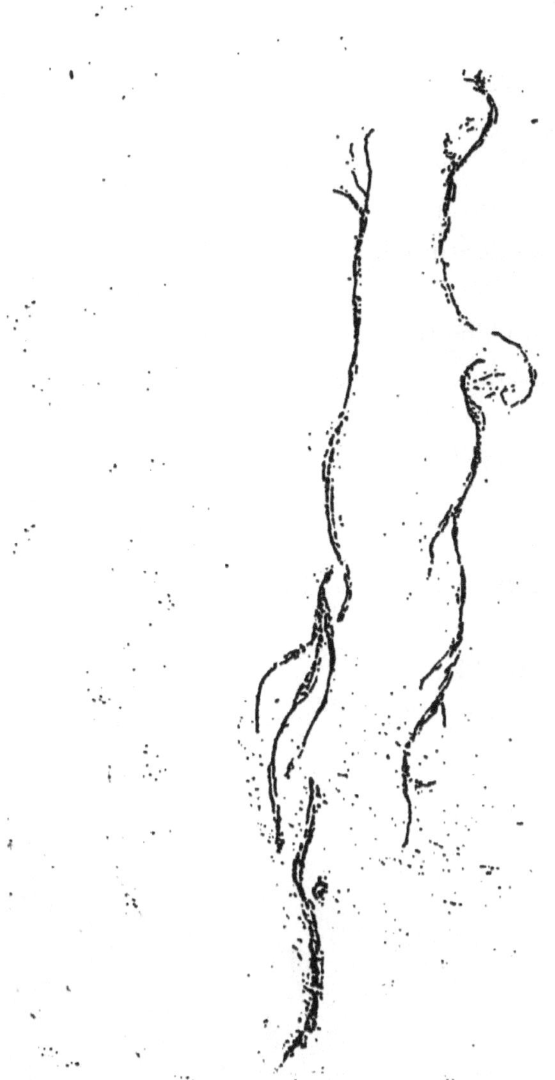

Rooms unfold
in the drift

Sunscript across the ceiling,
what stories does it tell?

A woman walking through the orchard
chanting as she breathes,

a light blue shell in the nest
empty and dry,

laughter in the rustling clouds.

Rooms unfold
and the dark condition fades.

Behind the roses
on the windowsill

two finches,
male and female,

meddle around in the seed
like nobody's business
and discuss
the qualities of love

that can be found
in sunflower, blueberry
and thistle.

To break the eye open
  and reveal what it cannot see

  a branch grows out of the spine
  and budding faces flower into wings.

  She walks between worlds
    and belongs to none.

  She is a crow
  when she wants meat,

  a cloud
  when she is thirsty.

  All of it hidden
where logic shatters

    into splintering twilight
    softly falling behind the retina.

  She is sanctuary
    when she glows.

When the idols crumble
  even darkness shines,

a gesture outward
    within and beyond
the skin, and skin against skin
more real than imagined.

Our weak physics
   cannot sustain such illumination
and the illusion of distance shatters.

  We falter in the making
and wake up blind –
    seeing the naked light at last

  and because of that failure
we surrender, abject, distant,
    a broken figure on the stage

  lost in the glare,
    the resplendent humility
of annihilation.

   Yet, somehow, comically
the figure remains.

She wrote in her diary,

"This is a book of dried flowers
without the flowers
    and more beautiful for it.

"I've studied them for days,
    changing invisible colors
    as I turned them through my fingers.

"I water them with tears
from the memory of my grandmother
    turning toward me on the cobblestone

whispering a word
    I live to hear."

In prayer
    I look
  into you

      but what
  are you
    and what
  am I?

How can
    there be
  two of us
      in this
  circumstance?

    I feel
      my own face
  but see
  the face
      of another

        in prayer
        moving
        outward.

Iridescence
on the billowing
   surface of a towering cloud –

mortality's
   anamnesis.

What was it?

So fleeting
and transliminal –

a crack in the window
where the soul escapes,
   so nearly perfect
      in its obscurity

I wept in your hair
when we embraced.

To realize
in the dissolving
        immediate,

    moss
 covering the rust
   on a shambling old
   railroad bridge

the way she
  cradled the coffee cup
in both hands
    and lifted it slowly
to her lips.

Splashes of rain
  in the birdbath,
  I recognize your voice.

  Delinquent charms
dangling in the branches
  of a cypress tree.

  One thing is another

  and we are walking together
  miles apart
    speaking softly
  repenting the distance
      like a river.

A cry from the marrow,

a pearl-eyed wolf
rushing you
out of your lover's dream.

Come to the brink.

The light,
  by mask of the world,

has destroyed
 every trace of itself.

Decay,
  by mask of the light

has destroyed
  the world.

(The willow
    beside grandmother's pond

  cannot be bent
    into a sepulcher.)

  The light
    enmeshed
in the leaves and branches
    cannot fade –

        becomes the seed
    through twilight and darkness

    of the morning,
    we, the dead,
      wait breathless
          arriving.

In the dim light
just before dawn
    the dead convene

    "Is this home?"

    "I don't think so,
but how are we to know
        disappearing and reappearing
    in every gust of wind?"

"So then, where are we?

    "We are at perpetual sunrise,
    caught in a synapse
    of flesh and breath."

    "I suppose so. The earth
is a red ribbed passenger
        caught in the sheets."

Closing my eyes
I see
        (whatever I am)
dense scratches
        the color of straw
    on a black field.

These things leaving
are not
   the crux
of the diamond.

   No ceiling,
    skyless

   I go
     wandering.

When you whisper
  into a world

 it leaves traces
in the worlds
   around you,

  impressions
  which are bodies themselves

 walking through
a field, mumbling
  half hymned fables

  of worlds
 you'll whisper tomorrow.

The house of death
is empty now

shuttered and crumbling
beneath the weight
of its compulsions.

All night
the starling weeps
just beyond the door.

If you wait inside
in perfect silence
long enough
for the starling
to grow wings
and leave the nest

resurrection will find you
both.

We were talking about
the death of complexity.

   "After a while,
    many years,
   you come to the
      end of it."

   "A generation
    passes
     in wilderness."

   "And you find
   someone not quite
      yourself, sitting
      on the porch steps,
      singing a low
        mumbling tune."

   "The equations
   are no longer important."

   "Someone is standing
      behind you,
   perhaps your spouse,
     or an old friend
       but you've never
   met her."

   "We are at the beginning.
   We can relax now."

"It is always before."

"Have you noticed
   how quiet we are?"

"Quiet and soft
as a reflection in a pool."

"The whole of it
 floods back
   so tenderly
that tears
   would dilute
 its gentle power."

"It is always before."

www.ingramcontent.com/pod-product-compliance
Lightning Source LLC
Chambersburg PA
CBHW020605160726
47991CB00002B/878